Romans Ruled

Written by Paul Perro
Illustrated by D.McRae

First published 2015

by hfk books

www.history-for-kids.com

All poems written by Paul Perro,
or Paul Perro and Jon Bratton.

By the same author in this series:
Great Greeks
Greek Myths

Contents

Introduction

The Romans used to rule the world
A long, long time ago.
They came from Rome in Italy
And spoke Latin, don't you know.

They were a great civilization
But also, as we shall see,
Roman rule could be harsh and cruel.
Let's find out more, shall we?

Famous Romans

Julius Caesar

You'll often hear about him in
A movie, book, or ballad.
He's the most famous Roman.
He even has a salad!
Yes, Caesar was a great man, but
He met a nasty end.
Stabbed, on the Ides of March,
In the back by a friend.

Pompey

He was so successful in battle
They nicknamed him "Pompey the Great"
But eventually he
Became Caesar's enemy
And soon he was "Pompey the Late"

Mark Antony

Mark Antony was Caesar's loyal friend
And he did avenge the great man's slaughter.
Then he fell in love with Cleopatra
The queen who bathed in milk (not water).

Augustus Caesar

Octavian had a bossy wife,
And he always tried to please her.
He made himself the emperor
And changed his name to Caesar

Caligula

There once was an Emperor Caligula -
He made a consul of his horse.
Historians agree
That obviously,
He was quite mad, of course.

Claudius

Claudius was a funny chap.
He limped and had a bad stammer.
But he'd wisdom and wit
Which made up for it.
His brain was more useful than glamour.

Nero

Emperor Nero liked music;
He liked to play the lyre.
One day he was playing it while
The city of Rome was on fire.
Nero was a terrible man -
He murdered his own step-brother.
He also chopped his wife's head off
And poisoned his own mother.

Romulus and Remus
- A Roman Myth

Romulus and Remus were twins
Their father was a god called "Mars"
Who had a planet named for him
And lots of chocolate bars.

They had a wicked uncle who
Threw them in the river to die.
But they were rescued by a wolf
Who happened to pass by.

The wolf pulled them from the river
And took them back home to her den.
She dried them off and fed them milk,
Until they were healthy again.

Before long a shepherd found them
And took them back home to his wife.
The couple raised them as their own,
A happy start to life.

The twins grew into big strong men.
Both leaders with lots of allies.
They planned to build a city where
The friendly wolf first heard their cries.

But the twins could not quite agree
On the exact location.
They had a nasty falling out,
A violent altercation.

And Romulus killed his brother
And very soon became
The king of the great city that
He named after his own name.

Yes, Romulus founded Rome,
It's where the name came from,
Although I've often wondered why
It's "Rome" instead of "Rom".

Spartacus

He was a soldier, then a slave,
Who famously led a revolt.
Spartacus took on the Romans,
And gave them quite a jolt.

It was while he was in training
In a school for gladiators -
Slaves forced to fight with each other
In the Roman amphitheatres.

None of these slaves wanted to die
A violent death in the coliseum
So when Spartacus did escape
He decided he would free 'em.

The escapees travelled around
Freeing slaves in other regions
Most gave their thanks and joined the ranks.
Together they fought off Roman legions.

The Romans sent a general
Named Crassus on a mission.
He was clever and he was tough
And he was quite a tactician.

So Crassus marched with his army
To take on the slave army, and
After a few battles
The Romans had the upper hand.

So Spartacus and his army
Went south, until they reached the sea.
Once there they asked some pirates to
Take them to Sicily.

Unfortunately however,
The wicked pirates betrayed them.
They did not give the slaves the ships
Even though they'd paid them.

The slaves were finally defeated
At The Battle of Siler River
Spartacus himself was killed
And the revolt crushed forever.

The battle was very bloody
And most of the slave army died.
More than 6000 prisoners
Were caught and crucified.

Today Spartacus is known as
A man of valour and conviction,
Even though his story ended
In defeat and crucifixion.

Hannibal

A military genius
(Or so most experts say)
He came from somewhere called Carthage
(Known as Tunisia today).

Hannibal fell out with the Romans
After he moved to Spain.
They quarrelled over territory;
He thought they were a pain.

Hannibal built up an army -
Thousands of soldiers, and
He even had some elephants
He'd brought from his homeland.

He marched them all to Italy,
A journey filled with dangers -
They crossed the Pyrenees and Alps
(Both massive mountain ranges).

But elephants can't climb mountains!
No way!" it's often muttered.
But yes, they can, because they are
Surprisingly sure-footed.

Once there he had hoped the locals
Would want to become his allies.
But they all seemed to think that
Fighting with Rome would be unwise.

So Hannibal and his army
Fought on nevertheless.
They were tactically astute and
They did have some success.

Despite winning some battles though,
They never conquered Rome,
And one day Hannibal got some
Disturbing news from home.

Apparently the Romans who'd
Seen Spain left unprotected,
Had conquered it, an outcome which
Our hero had not expected.

But that's not all, now Carthage too
Was under Roman attack.
Carthage was Hannibal's homeland
And so they all rushed back.

The Battle of Zama was where
The two armies would meet.
Unfortunately, for Hannibal
It ended in defeat.

What the Romans Did for Us

Roman roads were long and straight
You would not need much steering.
They really were a triumph of
Ancient engineering.

Now every schoolchild knows
About the Roman roads,
But Romans gave us so much more,
Yes, they invented loads.

Aqueducts – those big arched bridges
Which brought the water down
From the rivers in the hills
To the folk in town.

They gave us public libraries,
Great if you were a reader.
Before then books were hard to find -
There were no Kindles either.

The Romans built some public baths,
They built the sewers too.
Presumably, before they came,
The whole place smelled of poo!

They gave us apples, pears, and grapes,
Cabbages, turnips, carrots, peas.
Thanks to them we can now all eat
Our five-a-day with ease.

Glass for windows was another
Great invention of Rome's.
And central heating too keeps us
Warm inside our homes.

They invented the calendar,
It's just as well because
Without it you would never know
When your birthday was.

They gave us the police force and
Invented the street light.
Before then it was quite unsafe
To walk the streets at night.

In fashion, men wore the "toga" –
A big white woollen sheet;
It was draped from the shoulders to
The sandals on their feet.

So let's give thanks, they left behind
So much when they had gone.
And let us give thanks also that
Wearing togas never caught on.

Boudica

This is a tale of Boudica.
The Iceni Warrior Queen,
One of the most fearsome women
There has ever been.

She wore colourful clothes and she
Was tall and strong and loud.
She had a mane of long red hair.
You'd spot her in a crowd.

She and her husband the King ruled
A place where Norfolk is today.
The king made a deal with the Romans
And paid them to stay away.

When the king died though
Things did not go as planned.
The Romans decided to claim
All the king's wealth and land.

They came and stole from the Britons
Who were angry at being cheated.
What's more the Romans were violent -
The queen and her daughters mistreated.

Queen Boudica was quite outraged;
She had never been angrier.
She summoned all of the tribes to
A place now called East Anglia.

"We can't let them do this to us!"
She said, "It isn't right.
Let's get an army together
And let's give the Romans a fight!"

So all of the tribes joined forces,
They were led by the red-haired Queen
It was the biggest army that
Britain had ever seen.

Boudica's army marched around
And they attacked town after town.
Wherever they found Romans lived
They burned their houses down.

In the end though the Britons lost,
And the Romans were the winners.
The Romans were well-trained soldiers,
And the Britons, just beginners.

And Boudica's massive army
Suffered its final defeat
Well beaten by the Romans at
The Battle of Watling Street.

Yes Boudica lost in the end,
The Romans won, it's true,
But Boudica had scared them
And taught them a lesson or two.

Yes they regretted they'd crossed her,
They paid a price for being mean
To the Britons, and the princesses,
And the mighty Warrior Queen.

Pompeii

There once was a Roman city
And it was called Pompeii.
Disaster struck it in the year
79 Anno Domine.

Nearby there was a mountain and
Just in case you're curious,
I will tell you the mountain's name –
It was called Mount Vesuvius.

Except it wasn't a mountain
It was really a volcano,
A fact which the Pompeiians
Sadly did not know.

One August night it spewed out fire,
Lava, rocks - volcanic.
The Pompeiians were all afraid
And ran about in panic.

The city was destroyed that night
With heat and bangs and crashes
And buried under hundreds of tons
Of volcanic ashes.

Pompeii lay lost and forgotten
For hundreds and hundreds of years
Until the 1800s when
It was found by engineers.

They dug the ruins out and now
It's a tourist attraction today.
Every year millions
Visit ancient Pompeii.

Hadrian's Wall

When the Romans conquered Britain
Thousands of years ago.
They built towns in England and Wales,
They didn't want Scotland though.

The Scotsmen and the Romans
Did not get on at all.
To stop the Scots from stealing sheep
The Romans built a wall.

It stretched from Solway Firth in the west
To the Newcastle in the east.
To build it they used many stones,
Millions, at least.

The Emperor who was in charge,
(Hadrian was his name)
Did lots of things during his reign
But the wall gave him lasting fame.

It took fifteen years to build it,
Things took longer back then.
Hundreds of horses pulled the carts
There were thousands of working men.

They built forts and towers as well
They built them very tall,
So the Romans could see the Scots
Who tried to sneak up to the wall.

The Romans stayed in Britain for
Hundreds of years altogether.
I wonder why they stayed so long?
It couldn't have been the weather.

That the wall was built to last
Would be a fair thing to say.
It was built thousands of years ago
And is still standing today.

Indeed, from all around the world
People come to see it.
There's always a tourist around
You can almost guarantee it!

The Fall of Rome

The Mighty Roman Empire
For centuries all was well;
But nothing lasts for ever, and
Eventually it fell.

It had faced many big problems,
Like political corruption,
Slaves revolts, mad emperors,
Vesuvius's eruption.

They also suffered greatly with
Economic instability –
Lack of money caused by the
Tax-dodging nobility.

The biggest problem though, was
Invaders from abroad.
Goths, Huns and Vandals
Made up the barbarian horde.

The Empire fell for good when
Rome was attacked by Vandals.
That was the end of the Empire
Of Latin, togas and sandals.

Thank you for reading this book.

That's all I have to say for now.
This is the end; we're through.
I hope you have enjoyed these poems
And learned a thing or two.

THE END